Using Your Words

Talking It Out

Vanessa Flores

SOCIAL AND EMOTIONAL LEARNING FOR THE REAL WORLD™

Rosen Classroom™

How do you use your words?

Use your words to say how you feel.

Use your words to make friends.

Use your words to be kind.

Use your words to share ideas.

Use your words to work together!

Words to Know

friends